# Every Moment of Every Day

# Christine Marie Cocchiola, DSW, LCSW

© 2025, Coercive Control Consulting Institute, Inc. All rights reserved.
Published by Coercive Control Consulting Institute, Inc., Litchfield Hills, Connecticut
https://www.coercivecontrolconsulting.com/

**Every Moment of Every Day, by Christine Marie Cocchiola, DSW, LCSW**

ISBN 979-8-9994328-0-3 (paperback)
Library of Congress Control Number: 2025920488

Illustrating Concept by Christine Marie Cocchiola, DSW, LCSW
Illustration Artwork by Coby Bottoms

Publication managed by AuthorImprints.com

*Every Moment of Every Day* is a story about a girl and a boy a lot like you. Sometimes you have to go to your other parent's home. Sometimes you may be confused, and it may make you feel angry or sad. Sometimes even your body can tell you how you feel.

I hope this book helps you, even a little bit. And I hope it reminds you that your mama is always beside you, no matter how you feel, *every moment of every day.*

Sometimes
when it's time
to go...
I want to stay
right here
and spend
more time
with mom.

I want to read stories and have
our snuggle time.
My body tells me being here
at home feels safe and calm.

And sometimes when it's time to go, I may cry and get angry, but really I'm just sad.

My body feels uncomfortable—
my belly or my head,
or maybe it's another
part of me.
Something feels bad.

I want to pull mom closer.

Yet may push her away.

I'm confused,
and mom always
reminds me:
*My feelings are okay.*

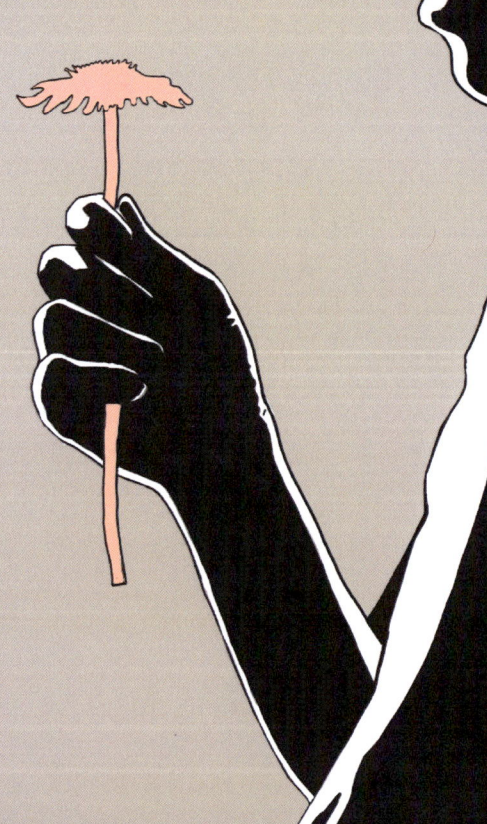

She lets me know
I can be myself,
and can show
how I feel here.

Mom will
respect my
boundaries,
and hug me
only if I want
her near.

She may sit close
and whisper...

Or show me with her smile
and tell me loud and clear:
*I love you endless
and always think of you*

*Even when you are away.*
*Every moment of every day.*

When you come back home, I'll be waiting here.

Mom can give you space or your favorite games we can play.

You can take a bath or we can go for a walk.

Mom can listen too, if sharing how you feel seems okay.

We can run around outside,
or even make a big
pillow tent and hide.

Or turn on some music
and dance.

Mom tells me:

*You get to choose our plans.*

And we will read stories,
and have our snuggle time too.

No matter where you are
and how you feel,
Mom's love is
unconditional and true.

And—

*I love you endless and always think of you.*
*Even when you are away.*
*Every moment of every day.*

# Acknowledgments

For Martin & Liv,
I am so grateful you found your trust in me.
You are my greatest teachers.
I love you more than the sun, the moon, and the stars in the sky,
and forever and a day.

For all children experiencing the distress outlined in this book:
May the path to freedom shine brightly and lead you back
everyday to the love of your safe, protective parent.

And for protective mamas everywhere:
This is the hardest work you will ever do—but you are the one to do it. You are
your children's greatest healer. Your brilliant light will show them a path towards
you—towards freedom—reigniting and fortifying their attachment to you .

# About the Author

Christine M. Cocchiola, DSW, LCSW is a recognized expert on coercive control who earned her doctorate from NYU under the mentorship of leading authority Dr. Evan Stark. She presents internationally on coercive control dynamics and developed The Protective Parenting Program, an evidence-based therapeutic model for parents whose children have been harmed by abusive partners. She coined the terms "malicious fracturing of attachment" and "disintegrated intuition" to describe children's experiences with abusive parents.

As both a survivor and a protective parent herself, Dr. Cocchiola hosts the *Perfect Prey* podcast and has authored books including the co-authored *Framed: Women in the Family Court Underworld*. Her expertise combines professional knowledge with lived experience to support both adult and child victims of coercive control, which she details in her TEDx talk "It is ALL Coercive Control." She makes her home in the Litchfield Hills of Connecticut.

Her forthcoming book *"Reignited Attachment: Healing Children of Coercive Control"* will be available in 2026.

www.ingramcontent.com/pod-product-compliance
Lightning Source LLC
Chambersburg PA
CBRC090842120626
46551CB00008B/730